Licia by Giles Fletcher

or Poems of Love in Honour of the Admirable and Singular Virtues of His Lady, to the Imitation of the Best Latin Poets and Others.

Giles Fletcher, the Elder, was born in Watford, Hertfordshire around 1548. His early life was spent at Cranbrook before he was sent to Eton in about 1561. From there, he went to King's College, Cambridge, and was appointed a fellow in 1568 and gained his B.A. in 1570.

Studying Greek and poetry, Fletcher contributed to the translation of several of Demosthenes' orations.

On 22 March 1572, Fletcher became a lecturer in King's and the following year he became a lecturer in Greek, a position which he held until Michaelmas term, 1579.

By 1581 Fletcher had risen to the post of dean of arts. However, Fletcher had decided to marry Joan Sheafe which meant relinquishing his fellowship.

Later returning to Cambridge he studied and received his Doctor of Civil Law degree after which the family settled back in Cranbrook.

On April 8th, 1582, Giles and Joan's first child, Phineas, was baptized. During the same year, Giles was made chancellor of the diocese of Sussex.

In 1584, Fletcher was elected for Winchelsea, one of the Cinque Ports, to the parliament which first sat on November 23rd.

London would now be their home. During his time in Parliament Fletcher served on three committees. In 1586, Fletcher was appointed as the Remembrancer of the City of London, an office which he held until 1605. In 1588 he was an ambassador to Russia to re-establish the treaty with Tsar Feodor I of Russia. Fletcher published a treatise, Of the Russe Common Wealth (1591). The treaty to be re-established was primarily concerning the English trade, but before he departed Queen Elizabeth made him a Master of Requests.

His sons, Phineas and Giles would both become poets in their own rights and continue the family's literary traditions.

Giles Fletcher, the Elder died in 1611.

Index of Contents

GILES FLETCHER – A SHORT BIOGRAPHY

I

Bright matchless star, the honour of the sky,
From whose clear shine heaven's vault hath all his light,
I send these poems to your graceful eye;
Do you but take them, and they have their right.
I build besides a temple to your name,
Wherein my thoughts shall daily sing your praise;
And will erect an altar for the same,
Which shall your virtues and your honour raise.
But heaven the temple of your honour is,
Whose brasen tops your worthy self made proud;
The ground an altar, base for such a bliss
With pity torn, because I sighed so loud.
And since my skill no worship can impart,
Make you an incense of my loving heart.
Sad all alone not long I musing sat,
But that my thoughts compelled me to aspire,
A laurel garland in my hand I gat;
So the Muses I approached the nigher.
My suite was this, a poet to become,
To drink with them, and from the heavens be fed.
Phoebus denied, and sware there was no room,
Such to be poets as fond fancy led.
With that I mourned and sat me down to weep.
Venus she smiled, and smiling to me said,
"Come, drink with me, and sit thee still and sleep."
This voice I heard; and Venus I obeyed.
That poison sweet hath done me all this wrong,
For now of love must needs be all my song.

II

Weary was love and sought to take his rest,
He made his choice, upon a virgin's lap;
And slyly crept from thence unto her breast,
Where still he meant to sport him in his hap;
The virgin frowned like Phoebus in a cloud;

"Go pack, sir boy, here is no room for such,
My breast no wanton foolish boy must shroud."
This said, my love did give the wag a touch;
Then as the foot that treads the stinging snake
Hastes to be gone, for fear what may ensue,
So love my love was forced for to forsake,
And for more speed, without his arrows flew.
"Pardon," he said, "For why? You seemed to me
My mother Venus in her pride to be."

III

The heavens beheld the beauty of my queen,
And all amazed, to wonder thus began:
"Why dotes not Jove, as erst we all have seen,
And shapes himself like to a seemly man?
Mean are the matches which he sought before,
Like bloomless buds, too base to make compare,
And she alone hath treasured beauty's store,
In whom all gifts and princely graces are."
Cupid replied: "I posted with the sun
To view the maids that livèd in those days,
And none there was that might not well be won,
But she, most hard, most cold, made of delays."
Heavens were deceived, and wrong they do esteem,
She hath no heat, although she living seem.

IV

Love and my love did range the forest wild,
Mounted alike, upon swift coursers both.
Love her encountered, though he was a child.
"Let's strive," saith he, whereat my love was wroth,
And scorned the boy, and checked him with a smile.
"I mounted am, and armèd with my spear;
Thou art too weak, thyself do not beguile;
I could thee conquer if I naked were."
With this love wept, and then my love replied:
"Kiss me, sweet boy, so weep my boy no more."
Thus did my love, and then her force she tried;
Love was made ice, that fire was before.
A kiss of hers, as I, poor soul, do prove,
Can make the hottest freeze and coldest love.

V

Love with her hair my love by force hath tied,
To serve her lips, her eyes, her voice, her hand;
I smiled for joy, when I the boy espied
To lie unchained and live at her command.
She if she look, or kiss, or sing, or smile,
Cupid withal doth smile, doth sing, doth kiss,
Lips, hands, voice, eyes, all hearts that may beguile,
Because she scorns all hearts but only this.
Venus for this in pride began to frown
That Cupid, born a god, enthralled should be.
She in disdain her pretty son threw down,
And in his place, with love she chainèd me.
So now, sweet love, though I myself be thrall,
Not her a goddess, but thyself I call.

VI

My love amazed did blush herself to see,
Pictured by art, all naked as she was.
"How could the painter know so much by me,
Or art effect what he hath brought to pass?
It is not like he naked me hath seen,
Or stood so nigh for to observe so much."
No, sweet; his eyes so near have never been,
Nor could his hands by art have cunning such;
I showed my heart, wherein you printed were,
You, naked you, as here you painted are;
In that my love your picture I must wear,
And show't to all, unless you have more care.
Then take my heart, and place it with your own;
So shall you naked never more be known.

VII

Death in a rage assaulted once my heart
With love of her, my love that doth deny.
I scorned his force, and wished him to depart,
I heartless was, and therefore could not die.
I live in her, in her I placed my life,
She guides my soul, and her I honour must.
Nor is this life but yet a living strife,
A thing unmeet, and yet a thing most just.
Cupid enraged did fly to make me love,
My heart lay guarded with those burning eyes
The sparks whereof denied him to remove;

So conquered now, he like a captive lies;
Thus two at once by love were both undone,
My heart not loved, and armless Venus' son.

VIII

Hard are the rocks, the marble, and the steel,
The ancient oak with wind and weather tossed;
But you, my love, far harder do I feel
Than flint, or these, or is the winter's frost.
My tears too weak, your heart they cannot move;
My sighs, that rock, like wind it cannot rent;
Too tiger-like you swear you cannot love;
But tears and sighs you fruitless back have sent.
The frost too hard, not melted with my flame,
I cinders am, and yet you feel no heat.
Surpass not these, sweet love, for very shame,
But let my tears, my vows, my sighs entreat;
Then shall I say as by trial find;
These all are hard, but you, my love, are kind.

IX

Love was laid down, all weary fast asleep,
Whereas my love his armor took away;
The boy awaked, and straight began to weep,
But stood amazed, and knew not what to say.
"Weep not, my boy," said Venus to her son,
"Thy weapons none can wield, but thou alone;
Licia the fair, this harm to thee hath done,
I saw her here, and presently was gone;
She will restore them, for she hath no need
To take thy weapons where thy valour lies;
For men to wound the Fates have her decreed,
With favour, hands, with beauty, and with eyes."
No, Venus, no: she scorns them, credit me;
But robbed thy son that none might care for thee.

X

A painter drew the image of the boy,
Swift love, with wings all naked, and yet blind;
With bow and arrows, bent for to destroy;
I blamed his skill, and fault I thus did find:
"A needless task I see thy cunning take;

Misled by love, thy fancy thee betrayed;
Love is no boy, nor blind, as men him make,
Nor weapons wears, whereof to be affrayed;
But if thou, love, wilt paint with greatest skill
A love, a maid, a goddess, and a queen;
Wonder and view at Licia's picture still,
For other love the world hath never seen;
For she alone all hope all comfort gives;
Men's hearts, souls, all, led by her favour lives."

XI

In Ida vale three queens the shepherd saw,
Queens of esteem, divine they were all three,
A sight of worth. But I a wonder shaw,
Their virtues all in one alone to be.
Licia the fair, surpassing Venus' pride,
(The matchless queen, commander of the gods,
When drawn with doves she in her pomp doth ride)
Hath far more beauty, and more grace by odds
Juno, Jove's wife, unmeet to make compare,
I grant a goddess, but not half so mild;
Minerva wise, a virtue, but not rare;
Yet these are mean, if that my love but smiled.
She them surpasseth, when their prides are full
As far as they surpass the meanest trull.

XII

I wish sometimes, although a worthless thing,
Spurred by ambition, glad to aspire,
Myself a monarch, or some mighty king,
And then my thoughts do wish for to be higher.
But when I view what winds the cedars toss,
What storms men feels that covet for renown,
I blame myself that I have wished my loss,
And scorn a kingdom, though it give a crown.
Ah Licia, though the wonder of my thought,
My heart's content, procurer of my bliss,
For whom a crown I do esteem as naught,
As Asia's wealth, too mean to buy a kiss!
Kiss me, sweet love, this favor do for me;
Then crowns and kingdoms shall I scorn for thee.

XIII

Enamored Jove commanding did entreat
Cupid to wound my love, which he denied,
And swore he could not for she wanted heat
And would not love, as he full oft had tried.
Jove in a rage, impatient this to hear,
Replied with threats; "I'll make you to obey!"
Whereat the boy did fly away for fear
To Licia's eyes, where safe intrenched he lay.
Then Jove he scorned, and dared him to his face,
For now more safe than in the heavens he dwelled,
Nor could Jove's wrath do wrong to such a place
Where grace and honour have their kingdom held.
Thus in the pride and beauty of her eyes
The seely boy the greatest god defies.

XIV

My love lay sleeping, where birds music made,
Shutting her eyes, disdainful of the light;
The heat was great but greater was the shade
Which her defended from his burning sight.
This Cupid saw, and came a kiss to take,
Sucking sweet nectar from her sugared breath;
She felt the touch, and blushed, and did awake,
Seeing t'was love, which she did think was death,
She cut his wings and causèd him to stay,
Making a vow, he should not thence depart,
Unless to her the wanton boy could pay
The truest, kindest and most loving heart.
His feathers still she usèd for a fan,
Till by exchange my heart his feathers won.

XV

I stood amazed, and saw my Licia shine,
Fairer than Phoebus, in his brightest pride,
Set forth in colors by a hand divine,
Where naught was wanting but a soul to guide.
It was a picture, that I could descry,
Yet made with art so as it seemed to live,
Surpassing fair, and yet it had no eye,
Whereof my senses could no reason give.
With that the painter bid me not to muse;
"Her eyes are shut, but I deserve no blame;
For if she saw, in faith, it could not choose

But that the work had wholly been a flame,"—
Then burn me, sweet, with brightness of your eyes,
That phoenix-like from thence I may arise.

XVI

Grant, fairest kind, a kiss unto thy friend!
A blush replied, and yet a kiss I had.
It is not heaven that can such nectar send
Whereat my senses all amazed were glad.
This done, she fled as one that was affrayed,
And I desired to kiss by kissing more;
My love she frowned, and I my kissing stayed,
Yet wished to kiss her as I did before.
Then as the vine the propping elm doth clasp,
Loath to depart till both together die,
So fold me, sweet, until my latest gasp,
That in thy arms to death I kissed may lie.
Thus whilst I live for kisses I must call;
Still kiss me, sweet, or kiss me not at all.

XVII

As are the sands, fair Licia, on the shore,
Or colored flowers, garlands of the spring,
Or as the frosts not seen, not felt before,
Or as the fruits that autumn forth doth bring;
As twinkling stars, the tinsel of the night,
Or as the fish that gallop in the seas;
As airs each part that still escapes our sight,
So are my sighs, controllers of my ease.
Yet these are such as needs must have an end,
For things finite none else hath nature done;
Only the sighs, which from my heart I send,
Will never cease, but where they first begun.
Accept them, sweet, as incense due to thee;
For you immortal made them so to be.

XVIII

I swear, fair Licia, still for to be thine,
By heart, by eyes, by what I held most dear;
Thou checked mine oath, and said: these were not mine,
And that I had no right by them to swear.
Then by my sighs, my passions, and my tears,

My vows, my prayers, my sorrow, and my love,
My grief, my joy, my hope, and hopeless fears,
My heart is thine, and never shall remove.
These are not thine, though sent unto thy view,
All else I grant, by right they are thine own;
Let these suffice that what I swear is true,
And more than this if that it could be known.
So shall all these though troubles ease my grief;
If that they serve to work in thee belief.

XIX

That time, fair Licia, when I stole a kiss,
From off those lips, where Cupid lovely laid,
I quaked for cold, and found the cause was this:
My life which loved, for love behind me staid.
I sent my heart my life for to recall,
But that was held, not able to return,
And both detained as captives were in thrall,
And judged by her, that both by sighs should burn.
Fair, burn them both, for that they were so bold,
But let the altar be within thy heart;
And I shall live because my life you hold,
You that give life, to every living part;
A flame I took whenas I stole the kiss;
Take you my life, yet can I live with this.

XX

First did I fear, when first my love began;
Possessed in fits by watchful jealousy,
I sought to keep what I by favour won,
And brooked no partner in my love to be.
But tyrant sickness fed upon my love,
And spread his ensigns, dyed with colour white;
Then was suspicion glad for to remove,
And loving much did fear to lose her quite.
Erect, fair sweet, the colors thou didst wear;
Dislodge thy griefs; the short'ners of content;
For now of life, not love, is all my fear,
Lest life and love be both together spent.
Live but, fair love, and banish thy disease,
And love, kind heart, both where and whom thou please.

XXI

Licia my love was sitting in a grove,
Tuning her smiles unto the chirping songs,
But straight she spied where two together strove,
Each one complaining of the other's wrongs.
Cupid did cry lamenting of the harm;
Jove's messenger, thou wrong'st me too too far;
Use thou thy rod, rely upon the charm;
Think not by speech my force thou canst debar.
A rod, Sir boy, were fitter for a child,
My weapons oft and tongue and mind you took;
And in my wrong at my distress thou smiled,
And scorned to grace me with a loving look.
Speak you, sweet love, for you did all the wrong
That broke his arrows, and did bind his tongue.

XXII

I might have died before my life begun,
Whenas my father for his country's good
The Persian's favor and the Sophy won
And yet with danger of his dearest blood.
Thy father, sweet, whom danger did beset,
Escapèd all, and for no other end
But only this, that you he might beget,
Whom heavens decreed into the world to send.
Then father, thank thy daughter for thy life,
And Neptune praise that yielded so to thee,
To calm the tempest when the storms were rife,
And that thy daughter should a Venus be.
I call thee Venus, sweet, but be not wroth;
Thou art more chaste, yet seas did favor both.

XXIII

My love was masked, and armèd with a fan,
To see the sun so careless of his light,
Which stood and gazed, and gazing waxèd wan
To see a star himself that was more bright.
Some did surmize she hid her from the sun,
Of whom in pride she scorned for to be kissed,
Or feared the harm by him to others done.
But these the reason of this wonder missed,
Nor durst the sun, if that her face were bare
In greatest pride, presume to take a kiss.
But she more kind did show she had more care

Than with her eyes eclipse him of his bliss.
Unmask you, sweet, and spare not; dim the sun;
Your light's enough, although that his were done.

XXIV

Whenas my love lay sickly in her bed,
Pale death did post in hope to have a prey;
But she so spotless made him that he fled;
"Unmeet to die," she cried, and could not stay.
Back he retired, and thus the heavens he told;
"All things that are, are subject unto me,
Both towns, and men, and what the world doth hold;
But her fair Licia still immortal be."
The heavens did grant; a goddess she was made,
Immortal, fair, unfit to suffer change.
So now she lives, and never more shall fade;
In earth a goddess, what can be more strange?
Then will I hope, a goddess and so near,
She cannot choose my sighs and prayers but hear.

XXV

Seven are the lights that wander in the skies,
And at these seven, I wonder in my love.
So see the moon, how pale she doth arise,
Standing amazed, as though she durst not move;
So is my sweet much paler than the snow,
Constant her looks, these looks that cannot change.
Mercury the next, a god sweet-tongued we know,
But her sweet voice doth wonders speak more strange.
The rising Sun doth boast him of his pride,
And yet my love is far more fair than he.
The warlike Mars can wieldless weapons guide,
But yet that god is far more weak than she.
The lovely Venus seemeth to be fair,
But at her best my love is far more bright.
Saturn for age with groans doth dim the air,
Whereas my love with smiles doth give it light.
Gaze at her brows, where heaven ingrafted is;
Then sigh, and swear, there is no heaven but this.

XXVI

I live, sweet love, whereas the gentle wind

Murmurs with sport in midst of thickest boughs,
Where loving woodbine doth the harbor bind,
And chirping birds do echo forth my vows;
Where strongest elm can scarce support the vine,
And sweetest flowers enameled have the ground;
Where Muses dwell; and yet hereat repine
That on the earth so rare a place was found.
But winds delight, I wish to be content;
I praise the woodbine, but I take no joy;
I moan the birds that music thus have spent;
As for the rest, they breed but mine annoy.
Live then, fair Licia, in this place alone;
Then shall I joy though all of these were gone.

XXVII

The crystal stream wherein my love did swim,
Melted in tears as partners of my woe;
Her shine was such as did the fountain dim,
The pearl-like fountain whiter than the snow;
Then like perfume, resolvèd with a heat,
The fountain smoked, as if it thought to burn;
A wonder strange to see the cold so great,
And yet the fountain into smoke to turn.
I searched the cause, and found it to be this:
She touched the water, and it burned with love.
Now by her means it purchased hath that bliss,
Which all diseases quickly can remove.
Then if by you these streams thus blessèd be,
Sweet, grant me love, and be not worse to me.

XXVIII

In time the strong and stately turrets fall,
In time the rose and silver lilies die,
In time the monarchs captive are and thrall,
In time the sea and rivers are made dry;
The hardest flint in time doth melt asunder;
Still living fame in time doth fade away;
The mountains proud we see in time come under;
And earth for age we see in time decay;
The sun in time forgets for to retire
From out the east where he was wont to rise;
The basest thoughts we see in time aspire,
And greedy minds in time do wealth despise.
Thus all, sweet fair, in time must have an end,

Except thy beauty, virtues, and thy friend.

XXIX

Why died I not whenas I last did sleep?
O sleep too short that shadowed forth my dear!
Heavens, hear my prayers, nor thus me waking keep!
For this were heaven, if thus I sleeping were.
For in that dark there shone a princely light;
Two milk-white hills, both full of nectar sweet,
Her ebon thighs, the wonder of my sight,
Where all my senses with their objects meet,—
I pass these sports, in secret that are best,
Wherein my thoughts did seem alive to be;
We both did strive, and weary both did rest;
I kissed her still, and still she kissèd me.
Heavens, let me sleep, and shows my senses feed,
Or let me wake and happy be indeed!

XXX

Whenas my Licia sailèd in the seas,
Viewing with pride god Neptune's stately crown,
A calm she made, and brought the merchant ease,
The storm she stayed, and checked him with a frown.
Love at the stern sate smiling and did sing
To see how seas had learned for to obey;
And balls of fire into the waves did fling;
And still the boy full wanton thus did say:—
"Both poles we burnt whereon the world doth turn,
The round of heaven from earth unto the skies;
And now the seas we both intend to burn,
I with my bow, and Licia with her eyes."
Then since thy force, heavens, earth, nor seas can move,
I conquered yield, and do confess I love.

XXXI

Whenas her lute is tunèd to her voice,
The air grows proud for honour of that sound,
And rocks do leap to show how they rejoice
That in the earth such music should be found.
Whenas her hair more worth, more pale than gold,
Like silver thread lies wafting in the air,
Diana-like she looks, but yet more bold;

Cruel in chase, more chaste and yet more fair.
Whenas she smiles, the clouds for envy breaks;
She Jove in pride encounters with a check;
The sun doth shine for joy whenas she speaks;
Thus heaven and earth do homage at her beck.
Yet all these graces, blots, not graces are,
If you, my love, of love do take no care.

XXXII

Years, months, days, hours, in sighs I sadly spend;
I black the night wherein I sleepless toss;
I love my griefs yet wish them at an end;
Thus time's expense increaseth but my loss.
I musing stand and wonder at my love,
That in so fair should be a heart of steel;
And then I think my fancy to remove,
But then more painful I my passions feel;
Thus must I love, sweet fair, until I die,
And your unkindness doth my love increase.
I conquered am, I can it not deny;
My life must end, yet shall my love not cease.
Then heavens, make Licia fair most kind to me,
Or with my life my loss may finished be!

XXXIII

I wrote my sighs, and sent them to my love;
I praised that fair that none enough could praise;
But plaints nor praises could fair Licia move;
Above my reach she did her virtues raise,
And thus replied: "False Scrawl, untrue thou art,
To feign those sighs that nowhere can be found;
For half those praises came not from his heart
Whose faith and love as yet was never found.
Thy master's life, false Scrawl shall be thy doom;
Because he burns, I judge thee to the flame;
Both your attempts deserve no better room."
Thus at her word we ashes both became.
Believe me, fair, and let my paper live;
Or be not fair, and so me freedom give.

XXXIV

Pale are my looks, forsaken of my life,

Cinders my bones, consumèd with thy flame,
Floods are my tears, to end this burning strife,
And yet I sigh for to increase the same;
I mourn alone because alone I burn;
Who doubts of this, then let him learn to love;
Her looks cold ice into a flame can turn,
As I distressèd in myself do prove.
Respect, fair Licia, what my torments are;
Count but the tithe both of my sighs and tears;
See how my love doth still increase my care,
And care's increase my life to nothing wears.
Send but a sigh my flame for to increase,
Or lend a tear and cause it so to cease.

XXXV

Whenas I wish, fair Licia, for a kiss
From those sweet lips where rose and lilies strive,
Straight do mine eyes repine at such a bliss,
And seek my lips thereof for to deprive;
Whenas I seek to glut mine eyes by sight,
My lips repine and call mine eyes away;
Thus both contend to have each other's right,
And both conspire to work my full decay.
O force admired of beauty in her pride,
In whose each part such strange effects there be,
That all my forces in themselves divide,
And make my senses plainly disagree.
If all were mine, this envy would be gone;
Then grant me all, fair sweet, or grant me none!

XXXVI

Hear how my sighs are echoed of the wind;
See how my tears are pitied by the rain;
Feel what a flame possessèd hath my mind;
Taste but the grief which I possess in vain.
Then if my sighs the blustering winds surpass,
And wat'ry tears the drops of rain exceed,
And if no flame like mine nor is nor was,
Nor grief like that whereon my soul doth feed,
Relent, fair Licia, when my sighs do blow;
Yield at my tears, that flintlike drops consume;
Accept the flame that doth my incense show,
Allow the grief that is my heart's perfume.
Thus sighs and tears, flame, grief shall plead for me;

So shall I pray, and you a goddess be.

XXXVII

I speak, fair Licia, what my torments be,
But then my speech too partial do I find;
For hardly words can with those thoughts agree,
Those thoughts that swarm in such a troubled mind.
Then do I vow my tongue shall never speak
Nor tell my grief that in my heart doth lie;
But cannon-like, I then surcharged do break,
And so my silence worse than speech I try.
Thus speech or none, they both do breed my care;
I live dismayed, and kill my heart with grief;
In all respects my case alike doth fare
To him that wants, and dare not ask relief.
Then you, fair Lucia, sovereign of my heart,
Read to yourself my anguish and my smart.

XXXVIII

Sweet, I protest, and seal it with an oath:
I never saw that so my thoughts did please;
And yet content displeased I see them wroth
To love so much and cannot have their ease.
I told my thoughts, my sovereign made a pause,
Disposed to grant, but willing to delay;
They then repined, for that they knew no cause,
And swore they wished she flatly would say nay.
Thus hath my love, my thoughts with treason filled,
And 'gainst my sovereign taught them to repine.
So thus my treason all my thoughts hath killed,
And made fair Licia say she is not mine.
But thoughts too rash my heart doth now repent;
And as you please, they swear, they are content.

XXXIX

Fair matchless nymph, respect but what I crave;
My thoughts are true, and honour is my love;
I fainting die whom yet a smile might save;
You gave the wound, and can the hurt remove.
Those eyes like stars that twinkle in the night,
And cheeks like rubies pale in lilies dyed,
Those ebon hands that darting hath such might

That in my soul my love and life divide,
Accept the passions of a man possessed;
Let love be loved and grant me leave to live;
Disperse those clouds that darkened have my rest,
And let your heaven a sun-like smile but give!
Then shall I praise that heaven for such a sun
That saved my life, whenas my grief begun.

XL

My grief begun, fair saint, when first I saw
Love in those eyes sit ruling with disdain,
Whose sweet commands did keep a world in awe,
And caused them serve your favor to obtain.
I stood as one enchanted with a frown,
Yet smiled to see all creatures serve those eyes,
Where each with sighs paid tribute to that crown,
And thought them gracèd by your dumb replies.
But I, ambitious, could not be content
Till that my service more than sighs made known;
And for that end my heart to you I sent
To say and swear that, fair, it is your own.
Then greater graces, Licia, do impart,
Not dumb replies unto a speaking heart.

SONNET MADE UPON THE TWO TWINS, DAUGHTERS OF THE LADY MOLLINEUX, BOTH PASSING LIKE, AND EXCEEDING FAIR

Poets did feign that heavens a Venus had,
Matchless herself, and Cupid was her son;
Men sued to these, and of their smiles were glad,
By whom so many famous were undone.
Now Cupid mourns that he hath lost his might,
And that these two so comely are to see;
And Venus frowns because they have her right.
Yet both so like that both shall blameless be;
With heaven's two twins for godhead these may strive,
And rule a world with least part of a frown;
Fairer than these two twins are not alive,
Both conquering queens, and both deserve a crown.
My thoughts presage, which time to come shall try,
That thousands conquered for their love shall die.

XLI

If, aged Charon, when my life shall end,
I pass thy ferry and my waftage pay,
Thy oars shall fall, thy boat and mast shall rend,
And through the deep shall be a dry foot-way.
For why? My heart with sighs doth breathe such flame
That air and water both incensèd be,
The boundless ocean from whose mouth they came,
For from my heat not heaven itself is free.
Then since to me thy loss can be no gain,
Avoid thy harm and fly what I foretell.
Make thou thy love with me for to be slain,
That I with her and both with thee may dwell.
Thy fact thus, Charon, both of us shall bless,
Thou save thy boat and I my love possess.

XLII

For if alone thou think to waft my love,
Her cold is such as can the sea command,
And frozen ice shall let thy boat to move,
Nor can thy forces row it from the land.
But if thou friendly both at once shalt take,
Thyself mayst rest. For why? My sighs will blow.
Our cold and heat so sweet a thaw shall make,
As that thy boat without thy help shall row.
Then will I sit and glut me on those eyes
Wherewith my life my eyes could never fill.
Thus from my boat that comfort shall arise,
The want whereof my life and hope did kill.
Together placed so thou her scorn shalt cross,
Where if we part thy boat must suffer loss.

XLIII

Are those two stars, her eyes, my life's light gone,
By which my soul was freèd from all dark?
And am I left distressed to live alone,
Where none my tears and mournful tale shall mark?
Ah sun, why shine thy looks, thy looks like gold,
When horsemen brave thou risest in the east?
Ah Cynthia pale, to whom my griefs I told,
Why do you both rejoice both man and beast?
And I alone, alone that dark possess
By Licia's absence brighter than the sun,
Whose smiling light did ease my sad distress,
And broke the clouds, when tears like rain begun.

Heavens, grant that light and so me waking keep,
Or shut my eyes and rock me fast asleep!

XLIV

Cruel fair love, I justly do complain
Of too much rigor and thy heart unkind,
That for mine eyes thou hast my body slain,
And would not grant that I should favour find.
I looked, fair love, and you my love looked fair,
I sighed for love and you for sport did smile.
Your smiles were such as did perfume the air,
And this perfumèd did my heart beguile.
Thus I confess the fault was in mine eyes,
Begun with sighs and ended with a flame.
I for your love did all the world despise;
And in these poems honored have your name.
Then let your love so with my fault dispense,
That all my parts feel not mine eyes' offense.

XLV

There shone a comet, and it was full west.
My thoughts presagèd what it did portend;
I found it threatened to my heart unrest,
And might in time my joys and comfort end.
I further sought and found it was a sun,
Which day nor night did never use to set.
It constant stood when heavens did restless run,
And did their virtues and their forces let.
The world did muse and wonder what it meant,
A sun to shine and in the west to rise;
To search the truth, I strength and spirits spent;
At length I found it was my Licia's eyes.
Now never after soul shall live in dark,
That hath the hap this western sun to mark.

XLVI

If he be dead, in whom no heart remains,
Or lifeless be in whom no life is found;
If he do pine that never comfort gains,
And be distressed that hath his deadly wound;
Then must I die whose heart elsewhere is clad,
And lifeless pass the greedy worms to feed;

Then must I pine that never comfort had,
And be distressed whose wound with tears doth bleed.
Which if I do, why do I not wax cold?
Why rest I not like one that wants a heart?
Why move I still like him that life doth hold,
And sense enjoy both of my joy and smart?
Like Niobe queen which made a stone did weep,
Licia my heart dead and alive doth keep.

XLVII

Like Memnon's rock, touched with the rising sun
Which yields a sound and echoes forth a voice,
But when it's drowned in western seas is done,
And drowsy-like leaves off to make a noise;
So I, my love, enlightened with your shine,
A poet's skill within my soul I shroud,
Not rude like that which finer wits decline,
But such as Muses to the best allowed.
But when your figure and your shape is gone
I speechless am like as I was before;
Or if I write, my verse is filled with moan,
And blurred with tears by falling in such store.
Then muse not, Licia, if my Muse be slack,
For when I wrote I did thy beauty lack.

XLVIII

I saw, sweet Licia, when the spider ran
Within your house to weave a worthless web,
You present were and feared her with your fan,
So that amazèd speedily she fled.
She in your house such sweet perfumes did smell,
And heard the Muses with their notes refined,
Thus filled with envy, could no longer dwell,
But straight returned and at your house repined.
Then tell me, spider, why of late I saw
Thee lose thy poison, and thy bowels gone;
Did these enchant and keep thy limbs in awe,
And made thy forces to be small or none?
No, no, thou didst by chance my Licia see,
Who for her look Minerva seemed to thee.

XLIX

If that I die, fair Licia, with disdain,
Or heartless live surprisèd with thy wrong,
Then heavens and earth shall accent both my pain,
And curse the time so cruel and so long.
If you be kind, my queen, as you are fair,
And aid my thoughts that still for conquest strive,
Then will I sing and never more despair,
And praise your kindness whilst I am alive.
Till then I pay the tribute of my tears,
To move thy mercy and thy constant truth.
Respect, fair love, how these with sorrow wears
The truest heart unless it find some ruth.
Then grace me, sweet, and with thy favor raise me,
So shall I live and all the world shall praise thee.

L

Ah Licia, sigh and say thou art my own;
Nay, be my own, as you full oft have said.
So shall your truth unto the world be known,
And I resolved where now I am afraid.
And if my tongue eternize can your praise,
Or silly speech increase your worthy fame,
If ought I can, to heaven your worth can raise,
The age to come shall wonder at the same.
In this respect your love, sweet love, I told,
My faith and truth I vowed should be forever.
You were the cause if that I was too bold;
Then pardon this my fault or love me never.
But if you frown I wish that none believe me,
For slain with sighs I'll die before I grieve thee.

LI

When first the sun whom all my senses serve,
Began to shine upon this earthly round,
The heavens for her all graces did reserve,
That Pandor-like with all she might abound.
Apollo placed his brightness in her eyes,
His skill presaging and his music sweet.
Mars gave his force; all force she now defies;
Venus her smiles wherewith she Mars did meet;
Python a voice, Diana made her chaste,
Ceres gave plenty, Cupid lent his bow,
Thetis his feet, there Pallas wisdom placed.
With these she queen-like kept a world in awe.

Yet all these honors deemèd are but pelf,
For she is much more worthy of herself.

LII

O sugared talk, wherewith my thoughts do live!
O brows, love's trophy and my senses' shine!
O charming smiles, that death or life can give!
O heavenly kisses from a mouth divine!
O wreaths too strong, and trammels made of hair!
O pearls inclosèd in an ebon pale!
O rose and lilies in a field most fair,
Where modest white doth make the red seem pale!
O voice whose accents live within my heart!
O heavenly hand that more than Atlas holds!
O sighs perfumed, that can release my smart!
O happy they whom in her arms she folds!
Now if you ask where dwelleth all this bliss,
Seek out my love and she will tell you this.

AN ODE

Love, I repent me that I thought
My sighs and languish dearly bought.
For sighs and languish both did prove
That he that languished sighed for love.
Cruel rigor, foe to state,
Looks disdainful, fraught with hate,
I did blame, but had no cause;
Love hath eyes, but hath no laws.
She was sad and could not choose
To see me sigh and sit and muse.
We both did love and both did doubt
Least any should our love find out.
Our hearts did speak, by sighs most hidden;
This means was left, all else forbidden.
I did frown her love to try,
She did sigh and straight did cry.
Both of us did sighs believe,
Yet either grievèd friend to grieve.
I did look and then did smile;
She left sighing all that while.
Both were glad to see that change,
Things in love that are not strange.
Suspicion, foolish foe to reason,
Causèd me seek to find some treason.

I did court another dame,
False in love, it is a shame!—
She was sorry this to view,
Thinking faith was proved untrue.
Then she swore she would not love
One whom false she once did prove.
I did vow I never meant
From promise made for to relent.
The more I said the worse she thought,
My oaths and vows were deemed as naught.
"False," she said "how can it be,
To court another yet love me?
Crowns and love no partners brook;
If she be liked I am forsook.
Farewell, false, and love her still,
Your chance was good, but mine was ill.
No harm to you, but this I crave,
That your new love may you deceive,
And jest with you as you have done,
For light's the love that quickly won."
"Kind, and fair-sweet, once believe me;
Jest I did but not to grieve thee.
Court I did, but did not love;
All my speech was you to prove.
Words and sighs and what I spent,
In show to her, to you were meant.
Fond I was your love to cross;
Jesting love oft brings this loss.
Forget this fault, and love your friend,
Which vows his truth unto the end."
"Content," she said, "if this you keep."
Thus both did kiss, and both did weep.
For women long they cannot chide,
As I by proof in this have tried.

A DIALOGUE BETWIXT TWO SEA-NYMPHS DORIS AND GALATEA CONCERNING POLPHEMUS; BRIEFLY TRANSLATED OUT OF LUCIAN

The sea-nymphs late did play them on the shore,
And smiled to see such sport was new begun,
A strife in love, the like not heard before,
Two nymphs contend which had the conquest won.
Doris the fair with Galate did chide;
She liked her choice, and to her taunts replied.

DORIS
Thy love, fair nymph, that courts thee on this plain,

As shepherds say and all the world can tell,
Is that foul rude Sicilian Cyclop-swain;
A shame, sweet nymph, that he with thee should mell.

GALATEA
Smile not, fair Doris, though he foul do seem,
Let pass thy words that savour of disgrace;
He's worth my love, and so I him esteem,
Renowned by birth, and come of Neptune's race,
Neptune that doth the glassy ocean tame,
Neptune, by birth from mighty Jove which came.

DORIS
I grant an honour to be Neptune's child,
A grace to be so near with Jove allied.
But yet, sweet nymph, with this be not beguiled;
Where nature's graces are by looks decried,
So foul, so rough, so ugly as a clown,
And worse than this, a monster with one eye!
Foul is not gracèd, though it wear a crown,
But fair is beauty, none can that deny.

GALATEA
Nor is he foul or shapeless as you say,
Or worse; for that he clownish seems to be,
Rough, satyr-like, the better he will play,
And manly looks the fitter are for me.
His frowning smiles are gracèd by his beard,
His eye-light, sun-like, shrouded is in one.
This me contents, and others make afeard.
He sees enough, and therefore wanteth none.

DORIS
Nay, then I see, sweet nymph, thou art in love,
And loving, dotes; and doting, dost commend
Foul to be fair; this oft do lovers prove;
I wish him fairer, or thy love an end.

GALATEA
Doris, I love not, yet I hardly bear
Disgraceful terms, which you have spoke in scorn.
You are not loved; and that's the cause I fear;
For why? My love of Jove himself was born.
Feeding his sheep of late amidst this plain,
Whenas we nymphs did sport us on the shore,
He scorned you all, my love for to obtain;
That grieved your hearts; I knew as much before.
Nay, smile not, nymphs, the truth I only tell,

For few can brook that others should excel.

DORIS
Should I envy that blind did you that spite?
Or that your shape doth please so foul a groom?
The shepherd thought of milk, you looked so white;
The clown did err, and foolish was his doom.
Your look was pale, and so his stomach fed;
But far from fair, where white doth want his red.

GALATEA
Though pale my look, yet he my love did crave,
And lovely you, unliked, unloved I view;
It's better far one base than none to have;
Your fair is foul, to whom there's none will sue.
My love doth tune his love unto his harp.
His shape is rude, but yet his wit is sharp.

DORIS
Leave off, sweet nymph, to grace a worthless clown.
He itched with love, and then did sing or say;
The noise was such as all the nymphs did frown,
And well suspected that some ass did bray.
The woods did chide to hear this ugly sound
The prating echo scorned for to repeat;
This grisly voice did fear the hollow ground,
Whilst artless fingers did his harpstrings beat.
Two bear-whelps in his arms this monster bore,
With these new puppies did this wanton play;
Their skins was rough but yet your loves was more;
He fouler was and far more fierce than they.
I cannot choose, sweet nymph, to think, but smile
That some of us thou fear'st will thee beguile.

GALATEA
Scorn not my love, until it can be known
That you have one that's better of your own.

DORIS
I have no love, nor if I had, would boast;
Yet wooed have been by such as well might speed:
But him to love, the shame of all the coast,
So ugly foul, as yet I have no need.
Now thus we learn what foolish love can do,
To think him fair that's foul and ugly too.

To hear this talk, I sat behind an oak,
And marked their words and penned them as they spoke.

AD LECTOREM, DISTICHON

CUJUSDAM DE AUTORE

Lascivi quaeres fuerit cur carminis autor:
Carmine lascivus, mente pudicus erat.

A LOVER'S MAZE

True are my thoughts, my thoughts that are untrue,
Blind are my eyes, my eyes that are not blind,
New is my love, my love that is not new,
Kind is that fair, that fair that is not kind.
Thus eyes and thoughts, that fairest fair, my love,
Blind and untrue, unkind, unconstant prove.

True are my thoughts because they never flit,
Untrue my thoughts because they me betrayed;
Blind are my eyes because in clouds I sit,
Not blind my eyes because I looks obeyed.
Thus eyes and thoughts, my dearest fair may view
In sight, in love, not blind, nor yet untrue.

New is my love because it never dies,
Old is my love because it ever lives;
Kind is that fair because it hate denies,
Unkind that fair because no hope it gives.
Thus new my love, and still that fair unkind,
Renews my love, and I no favour find.

Sweet are my dreams, my dreams that are not sweet,
Long are the nights, the nights that are not long,
Meet are the pangs, these pangs that are unmeet,
Wronged is my heart, my heart that hath no wrong.
Thus dreams, and night, my heart, my pangs, and all
In taste, in length, conspire to work my fall.

Sweet are my dreams because my love they show,
Unsweet my dreams because but dreams they are;
Long are the nights because no help I know,
Meet are the nights because they end my care.
Thus dreams and nights wherein my love take sport,
Are sweet, unsweet, are long, and yet too short.

Meet are my pangs because I was too bold,

Unmeet my pangs because I loved so well;
Wronged was my heart because my grief it told,
Not wronged. For why? My grief it could not tell.
Thus you my love unkindly cause this smart,
That will not love to ease my pangs and heart.

Proud is her look, her look that is not proud,
Done all my days, my days that are not done,
Loud are my sighs, my sighs that are not loud,
Begun my death, my death not yet begun.
Thus looks and days and sighs and death might move
So kind, so fair, to give consent to love.

Proud is her look because she scorns to see,
Not proud her look for none dare say so much;
Done are my days because they hapless be,
Not done my days because I wish them such.
Thus looks and days increase this loving strife.
Not proud, nor done, nor dead, nor giving life.

Loud are my sighs because they pierce the sky,
Not loud my sighs because they are not heard;
My death begun because I artless cry,
But not begun because I am debarred.
Thus sighs and death my heart no comfort give;
Both life deny, and both do make me live.

Bold are her smiles, her smiles that are not bold,
Wise are her words, those words that are not wise,
Cold are her lips, those lips that are not cold,
Ice are those hands, those hands that are not ice.
Thus smiles and words, her lips, her hands, and she,
Bold, wise, cold, ice, love's cruel torments be.

Bold are her smiles, because they anger slay,
Not bold her smiles because they blush so oft;
Wise are her words because they wonders say,
Not wise her words because they are not soft.
Thus smiles and words, so cruel and so bold,
So blushing wise, my thoughts in prison hold.

Cold are her lips because they breathe no heat,
Not cold her lips because my heart they burn;
Ice are her hands because the snow's so great,
Not ice her hands that all to ashes turn.
Thus lips and hands cold ice my sorrow brew;
Hands, warm white snow and lips cold cherry-red.

Small was her waist, the waist that was not small,
Gold was her hair, the hair that was not gold,
Tall was her shape, the shape that was not tall;
Folding the arms, the arms that did not fold.
Thus hair and shape, those folding arms and waist,
Did make me love, and loving made me waste.

Small was her waist, because I could it span,
Not small her waist because she wanted all;
Gold was her hair because a crown it wan,
Not gold her hair because it was more pale.
Thus smallest waist, the greatest waste doth make,
And finest hair most fast a lover take.

Tall was her shape because she touched the sky,
Not tall her shape because she comely was;
Folding her arms because she hearts could tie,
Not folded arms because all bands they pass.
Thus shape and arms with love my heart did ply,
That hers I am, and must be till I die.

Sad was her joy, her joy that was not sad,
Short was her stay, her stay that was not short,
Glad was her speech, her speech that was not glad,
Sporting those toys, those toys that were not sport.
Thus was my heart with joy, speech, toys and stay,
Possessed with love, and so stol'n quite away.

Sad was her joy because she did respect,
Not sad her joy because her joy she had,
Short was her stay because to small effect,
Long was her stay because I was so sad.
Thus joy and stay, both crossed a lover's sport,
The one was sad, the other too too short.

Glad was her speech because she spake her mind,
Not glad her speech because afraid to speak;
Sporting her toys because my love was kind,
Not toys in sport because my heart they break.
Thus speech and toys my love began in jest;
Sweet, yield to love, and make thy servant blest.

Tread you the maze, sweet love, that I have run,
Mark but the steps which I imprinted have;
End but your love whereas my thoughts begun;
So shall I joy and you a servant have.
If not, sweet love, then this my suit deny;
So shall you live, and so your servant die.

AN ELEGY

I

Down in a bed and on a bed of down,
Love, she, and I to sleep together lay;
She like a wanton kissed me with a frown,
Sleep, sleep, she said, but meant to steal away;
I could not choose but kiss, but wake, but smile,
To see how she thought us two to beguile.

She feigned a sleep, I waked her with a kiss;
A kiss to me she gave to make me sleep;
If I did wrong, sweet love, my fault was this,
In that I did not you thus waking keep.
"Then kiss me, sweet, that so I sleep may take,
Or let me kiss to keep you still awake."

The night drew on and needs she must be gone;
She wakèd Love, and bid him learn to wait;
She sighed, she said, to leave me there alone,
And bid Love stay but practise no deceit.
Love wept for grief, and sighing made great moan,
And could not sleep nor stay if she were gone.

"Then stay, sweet love;" a kiss with that I gave;
She could not stay, but gave my kiss again;
A kiss was all that I could get or crave,
And with a kiss she bound me to remain.
"Ah Licia," still I in my dreams did cry,
"Come, Licia, come, or else my heart will die."

II

Distance of place my love and me did part,
Yet both did swear we never would remove;
In sign thereof I bid her take my heart,
Which did, and doth, and can not choose but love.
Thus did we part in hope to meet again,
Where both did vow most constant to remain.

A she there was that passed betwixt us both,
By whom each knew how other's cause did fare;
For men to trust men in their love are loth;
Thus had we both of love a lover's care.

Haply he seeks his sorrows to renew,
That for his love doth make another sue.

By her a kiss, a kiss to me she sent.
A kiss for price more worth than purest gold.
She gave it her, to me the kiss was meant;
A she to kiss, what harm if she were bold?
Happy those lips that had so sweet a kiss,
For heaven itself scarce yields so sweet a bliss!

This modest she, blushing for shame of this,
Or loth to part from that she liked so well,
Did play false play, and gave me not the kiss;
Yet my love's kindness could not choose to tell.
Then blame me not, that kissing sighed and swore
I kissed but her whom you had kissed before.

Sweet, love me more, and blame me not, sweet love;
I kissed those lips, yet harmless I do vow;
Scarce would my lips from off those lips remove,
For still methought, sweet fair, I kissèd you.
And thus, kind love, the sum of all my bliss
Was but begun and ended in a kiss.

Then send me more, but send them by your friend;
Kiss none but her, nor her, nor none at all.
Beware by whom such treasures you do send,
I must them lose except I for them call.
And love me, dear, and still still kissing be;
Both like and love, but none, sweet love, but me.

III

If sad complaint would show a lover's pain,
Or tears express the torments of my heart,
If melting sighs would ruth and pity gain,
Or true laments but ease a lover's smart;

Then should my plaints the thunder's noise surmount,
And tears like seas should flow from out my eyes;
Then sighs like air should far exceed all count,
And true laments with sorrow dim the skies.

But plaints and tears, laments and sighs I spend,
Yet greater torments do my heart destroy;
I could all these from out my heart still send,
If after these I might my love enjoy.

But heavens conspire, and heavens I must obey,
That seeking love I still must want my ease;
For greatest joys are tempered with delay,
Things soon obtained do least of all us please.

My thoughts repine and think the time too long,
My love impatient wisheth to obtain;
I blame the heavens that do me all this wrong
To make me loved and will not ease my pain.

No pain like this, to love and not enjoy;
No grief like this, to mourn and not be heard;
No time so long as that which breeds annoy;
No hell like this, to love and be deferred!

But heaven shall stand and earth inconstant fly,
The sun shall freeze and ice inconstant burn,
The mountains flow and all the earth be dry,
Ere time shall force my loving thoughts to turn.

Do you resolve, sweet love, to do the same,
Say that you do, and seal it with a kiss.
Then shall our truths the heavens' unkindness blame
That can not hurt yet show their spite in this.

The silly 'prentice bound for many years,
Doth hope that time his service will release;
The town beseiged that lives in midst of fears,
Doth hope in time the cruel wars will cease.

The toiling plough-man sings in hope to reap,
The tosséd bark expecteth for a shore;
The boy at school to be at play doth leap,
And straight forgets the fear he had before.

If those by hope do joy in their distress,
And constant are in hope to conquer time,
Then let not hope in us, sweet friend, be less,
And cause our love to wither in the prime.

Let me conspire and time will have an end,
So both of us in time shall have a friend.

FINIS.

Giles Fletcher, author of Licia, was one of that distinguished family that included Richard Fletcher, the Bishop of London, and his son John Fletcher, the dramatist. The two sons of Dr. Giles Fletcher were also men of marked poetic ability: Phineas, the author of that extraordinary allegorical poem, The Purple Island; and Giles, of Christ's Victory and Triumph. There was a strong family feeling in this circle; Phineas and Giles pay compliments to each other in their verse and show great reverence and tenderness toward the memory of the poetic powers of their father. But Giles Fletcher the elder was not thought of in his own time as a poet. Educated at Eton and Trinity, Cambridge, where he was made LL.D. in 1581, a member of Parliament in '85, employed in many public services at home and abroad during a career that lasted until 1611, in which year Dr. Fletcher died at the age of seventy-two, he was known as a man of action, a man for public responsibility, rather than as the retired scholar or riming courtier. Most important among the foreign embassages undertaken by Fletcher was the one to Russia. The results were of great import to England, commercially and otherwise, but the book he wrote on his return was, for political reasons, suppressed.

It happened that the years of enforced idleness that followed the suppression of this book came in the time when the young sonneteers at London were all busy. He returned from his embassage in '89; the book was suppressed in '91. Licia was published in '93. The writing of Licia was "rather an effect than a cause of idleness;" he did it "only to try his humor," he says apologetically in the dedicatory addresses. "Whereas my thoughts and some reasons drew me rather to have dealt in causes of greater weight, yet the present jar of this disagreeing age drives me into a fit so melancholy, as I had only leisure to grow passionate."

In case wise heads should think him to be treating "an idle subject and so frivolous," or that it has been "vainly handled and so odious," he sets forth the nobility of his view. "Howsoever, Love in this age hath behaved himself in that loose manner as it is counted a disgrace to give him but a kind look, yet I take the passion in itself to be of that honor and credit, as it is a perfect resemblance of the greatest happiness, and rightly valued at his just price (in a mind that is sincerely and truly amorous), an affection of greatest virtue and able of himself to eternise the meanest vassal." "For Love," he declares, "is a goddess (pardon me though I speak like a poet) not respecting the contentment of him that loves, but the virtues of the beloved; satisfied with wondering, fed with admiration; respecting nothing but his lady's worthiness; made as happy by love as by all favors; chaste by honor; far from violence; respecting but one, and that one in such kindness, honesty, truth, constancy, and honor, as were all the world offered to make a change, yet the boot were too small and therefore bootless. This is love, and far more than this, which I know a vulgar head, a base mind, an ordinary conceit, a common person will not nor cannot have.
Thus do I commend that love wherewith in these poems I have honoured the worthy Licia."

The sonnet-cycle is inscribed "To the worthie kinde wise and virtuous ladie, the Ladie Mollineux; wife to the right worshipful Sir Richard Mollineux Knight." Nothing is known of this lady, except that her family may possibly have been very distantly connected with that of Fletcher. What the poet's feeling was towards his patroness he defines sufficiently. "Now in that I have written love sonnets, if any man measure my affection by my style, let him say I am in love.... Yet take this by the way; though I am so liberal to grant thus much, a man may write of love and not be in love, as well as of husbandry and not go to the plough, or of witches and be none, or of holiness and be flat profane."

What "shadowings" the poet may intend he refuses to confide to us. "If thou muse what my Licia is, take her to be some Diana, at the least chaste; or some Minerva; no Venus, fairer far. It may be she is Learning's image, or some heavenly wonder, which the precisest may not dislike: perhaps under that name I have shadowed Discipline. It may be I mean that kind courtesy which I found at the patroness of these poems. It may be some college; it may be my conceit, and portend nothing." It is evident then that the patroness herself is not the real person behind the poetic title. He therefore dedicates Licia to Lady Molineux, not because the sonnets themselves are addressed to her, but because he has received "favours undeserved" at her hands and those of "wise Sir Richard" for which he "wants means to make recompence," and therefore in the meantime he begs her to accept this. "If thou like it," he says to the reader, "take it, and thank the worthy Lady Mollineux, for whose sake thou hast it; worthy, indeed, and so not only reputed by me in private affection of thankfulness but so equally to be esteemed by all that know her. For if I had not received of her ... those unrequitable favours, I had not thus idly toyed."

A warm admirer of Fletcher has expressed his opinion that Licia "sparkles with brilliants of the first water." A more temperate judgment is that of another, who says that he "took part without discredit in the choir of singers who were men of action too." Licia is what a typical sonnet-cycle ought to be, a delicate and almost intangible thread of story on which are strung the separate sonnet-pearls. In this case the jewels have a particular finish. Fletcher has adopted the idea of a series of quatrains, often extending the number to four, and a concluding couplet, which he seems fond of utilising to give an epigrammatic finish to the ingenious incident he so often makes the subject of the sonnet. He is fully in the spirit of the Italian mode, however, acknowledging in his title page his indebtedness to poets of other nationalities than his own.